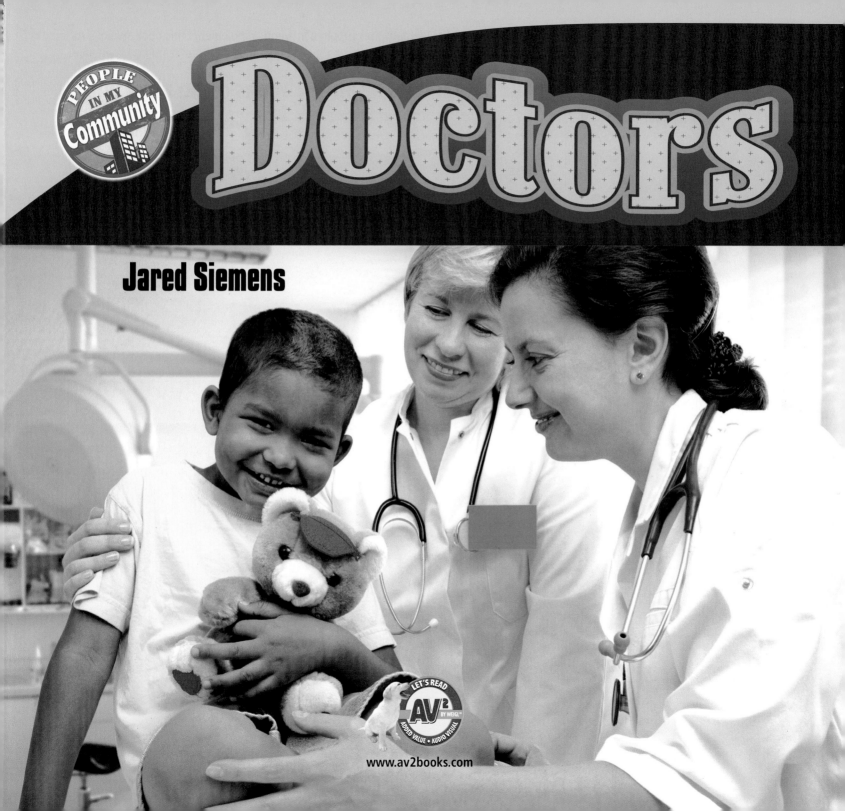

Doctors

PEOPLE IN MY Community

Jared Siemens

LET'S READ

AV²

BY WEIGL™

ADDED VALUE • AUDIO VISUAL

Go to www.av2books.com, and enter this book's unique code.

BOOK CODE

G973563

AV² by Weigl brings you media enhanced books that support active learning.

AV² provides enriched content that supplements and complements this book. Weigl's AV² books strive to create inspired learning and engage young minds in a total learning experience.

Your AV² Media Enhanced books come alive with...

Audio
Listen to sections of the book read aloud.

Video
Watch informative video clips.

Embedded Weblinks
Gain additional information for research.

Try This!
Complete activities and hands-on experiments.

Key Words
Study vocabulary, and complete a matching word activity.

Quizzes
Test your knowledge.

Slide Show
View images and captions, and prepare a presentation.

... and much, much more!

Published by AV² by Weigl
350 5ᵗʰ Avenue, 59ᵗʰ Floor New York, NY 10118
Websites: www.av2books.com   www.weigl.com

Library of Congress Cataloging-in-Publication Data

Siemens, Jared.
 Doctors / Jared Siemens.
      pages cm. -- (People in my community)
 Includes bibliographical references and index.
 ISBN 978-1-4896-3641-6 (hard cover : alk. paper) -- ISBN 978-1-4896-3642-3 (soft cover : alk. paper)
 ISBN 978-1-4896-3643-0 (single user ebook) -- ISBN 978-1-4896-3644-7 (multi-user ebook)
 1. Physicians--Juvenile literature. 2. Medical care--Juvenile literature. I. Title.
 R690.S523 2015
 610.69'5--dc23
                                      2015002648

Printed in the United States of America in Brainerd, Minnesota
1 2 3 4 5 6 7 8 9 0 19 18 17 16 15

022015
WEP270215

Project Coordinator: Jared Siemens
Design: Mandy Christiansen

Every reasonable effort has been made to trace ownership and to obtain permission to reprint copyright material. The publishers would be pleased to have any errors or omissions brought to their attention so that they may be corrected in subsequent printings.

Weigl acknowledges iStock and Getty Images as the primary image suppliers for this title.

Doctors

CONTENTS

People who live close together are part of a community.

The doctor is a person in my community.

A doctor works in a hospital.

People go to hospitals
when they are sick or hurt.

A doctor works to find out why I am sick.

She helps me get well by giving me medicine.

The doctor makes sure everything in my body is working right.

He weighs and measures me to see if I am growing as much as I should be.

The doctor uses a tool that tells her how hot or cold I am.

She also listens to my heart and lungs with a special tool.

The doctor helps
me to stay healthy.

She uses medicine to keep me from getting sick.

The doctor looks at pictures made by a special camera.

These pictures show her the inside of my body.

Doctors operate to fix problems people have with their bodies.

Doctors are an important part of my community.

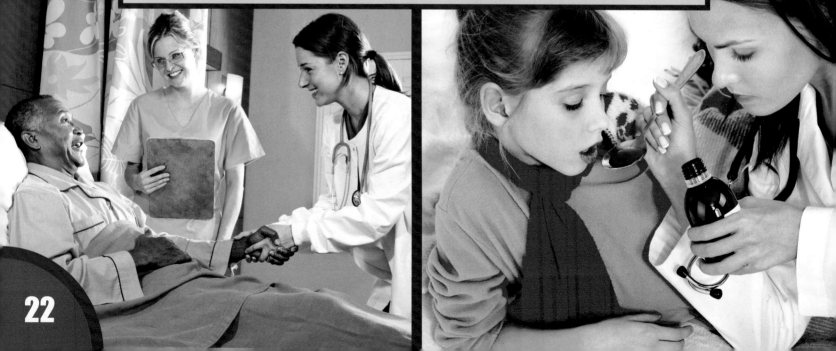

See what you have learned about the doctor.

Describe what you see in each of the pictures.

KEY WORDS

Research has shown that as much as 65 percent of all written material published in English is made up of 300 words. These 300 words cannot be taught using pictures or learned by sounding them out. They must be recognized by sight. This book contains 59 common sight words to help young readers improve their reading fluency and comprehension. This book also teaches young readers several important content words, such as proper nouns. These words are paired with pictures to aid in learning and improve understanding.

Page	Sight Words First Appearance
4	a, are, close, live, of, part, people, together, who
5	in, is, my, the
6	works
7	go, or, they, to, when
8	am, find, I, out, why
9	by, get, helps, me, she, well
10	makes, right
11	and, as, be, he, if, much, see, should
12	her, how, tells, that, uses
13	also, with
15	from, keep
16	at, looks, made, pictures
17	show, these
18	have, their
21	an, important

Page	Content Words First Appearance
4	community
5	doctor, person
6	hospital
9	medicine
10	body, everything
12	tool
13	heart, lungs
16	camera
18	problems